CULTURES CONNECT US!

# LEGENDS

BY CYRIL BASSINGTON

Gareth Stevens
PUBLISHING

Please visit our website, www.garethstevens.com. For a free color catalog of all our high-quality books, call toll free 1-800-542-2595 or fax 1-877-542-2596.

**Cataloging-in-Publication Data**

Names: Bassington, Cyril.
Title: Legends / Cyril Bassington.
Description: New York : Gareth Stevens Publishing, 2020. | Series: Cultures connect us! | Includes glossary and index.
Identifiers: ISBN 9781538238424 (pbk.) | ISBN 9781538238448 (library bound) | ISBN 9781538238431 (6 pack)
Subjects: LCSH: Legends–Juvenile literature. | Urban folklore–Juvenile literature.
Classification: LCC GR78.B374 2020 | DDC 398.2–dc23

Published in 2020 by
**Gareth Stevens Publishing**
111 East 14th Street, Suite 349
New York, NY 10003

Designer: Reann Nye
Editor: Therese Shea

Photo credits: series art (background) Lukasz Szwaj/Shutterstock.com; cover, p. 1 Nando Machado/Shutterstock.com; p. 5 Alex Kravtsov/Shutterstock.com; p. 7 Tutti Frutti/Shutterstock.com; p. 9 duncan1890/DigitalVision Vectors/Getty Images; p. 11 Bettmann/Getty Images; p. 13 Gilmanshin/Shutterstock.com; p. 15 ZU_09/DigitalVision Vectors/Getty Images; p. 17 Fotokostic/Shutterstock.com; p. 19 Hitdelight/Shutterstock.com; p. 21 Monkey Business Images/Shutterstock.com.

Printed in the United States of America

CPSIA compliance information: Batch #CS19GS: For further information contact Gareth Stevens, New York, New York at 1-800-542-2595.

# CONTENTS

**Boldface** words appear in the glossary.

# What a Legend!

Some sports stars are called legends. That means they're so skilled that people will remember them for many years to come. Certain stories that have been passed down for many years are also called legends. All **cultures** have legends.

# Not All True

Legends are told like they're history. They're usually about a real person or place. However, they're probably not all true. Robin Hood is a legend from England. He might have been a real person, but many stories about him are made up.

7

# A Teaching Tool

Legends often **reflect** values. The Robin Hood legend comes from a time when poor people suffered under unjust British laws. Robin robs from the rich and gives to the poor. People who valued the rights of the poor passed on the stories.

9

We know George Washington was real, but the story of young Washington chopping down his father's cherry tree is a legend. In the legend, he **confesses** what he did. This American tale reminds us it's **admirable** to be truthful.

11

# Older Legends

Some legends are even older. They were only spoken at first. Later, they were written down. The legend of King Arthur is one of these stories. Arthur may or may not have been a real ruler in England. His stories spread the values of **chivalry**.

13

The Greek **epic** the *Iliad* was told long before it was written down—over 2,000 years ago! It's about a war between the ancient city of Troy and the Greeks. This likely happened, though many heroes in the legend didn't exist.

15

## Legends Across Cultures

Some legends are alike across many cultures. For example, many peoples told stories of giants, dragons, and sea monsters. Scientists think all these are based on real-life creatures. For example, people may have dreamed up dragons after finding dinosaur bones!

17

# Urban Legends

Legends don't have to be old, though. There might be legends in your community about a spooky old house or graveyard. These are sometimes called urban legends. They're often not written down but are passed on by word of mouth.

19

## Pass It On

Is there a story that has been passed down in your family? Does it have some **details** that seem like the truth but also some parts that probably didn't happen? Keep passing it on. It might become a legend!

# GLOSSARY

**admirable:** very good

**chivalry:** the system of values, such as loyalty and honor, that knights in the Middle Ages were expected to follow

**confess:** to tell the bad things one has done

**culture:** the beliefs and ways of life of a group of people

**detail:** a small part of something

**epic:** a long poem that tells the story of a hero's adventures

**reflect:** to show something or make it known

# FOR MORE INFORMATION

## BOOKS

Latchana, Karen Kenney. *Spine-Tingling Urban Legends*. Minneapolis, MN: Lerner Publications, 2018.

Randolph, Joanne, ed. *The Myths and Legends of the First Peoples of the Americas*. New York, NY: Cavendish Square Publishing, 2018.

Shea, Therese. *Fables, Myths, and Legends*. New York, NY: Enslow Publishing, 2019.

## WEBSITES

### Native American Indian Legends and Folklore
*www.native-languages.org/legends.htm*
Find links to legends that tell you about the cultures of Native American peoples.

### What Is a Legend?
*greece.mrdonn.org/legends.html*
Read more about Greek legends, and learn the famous legend of the Trojan horse.

# INDEX